Lilies

Introduction by Scott D. Appell

MetroBooks

INTRODUCTION

Within the garden's peaceful scene
Appear'd two lovely foes,
Aspiring to the rank of queen,
The Lily and the Rose.

WILLIAM COWPER

Paired in countless gardens and a multitude of verses, the lily and the rose have long vied for position as the world's favorite flower. Here, then, is a volume that celebrates the candidacy of the lily for that esteemed title and explores the rich variety of shapes, colors, and forms of this regal bloom.

The genus *Lilium* comprises about one hundred species of perennial, often fragrant-flowered, bulbs, with hybrids, selections, sports, and cultivars numbering well into the thousands. Lilies are, indeed, among our most cherished (and easily recognized) summer- and early autumn–blooming garden subjects, beloved by novice gardeners and professional horticulturists alike.

Taxonomists and botanical etymologists disagree about the origin of the genus name *Lilium*, which many presume to be derived from the Celtic *lis*, or *li*, which translates as "water"—an allusion to the white color of *Lilium candidum*. Another possible source is the name Laelia, one of the Vestal virgins, which may have been used to suggest the delicacy of lily flowers. The common name "lily" may have eastern origins. The Egyptian word *hrr-t*, pronounced *hl-eli* or *hr-eri*, may have evolved (by way of Greek or Latin) into *lilium*, which was subsequently passed on in various forms throughout Europe. It is also possible that the Greek word *leiron*, derived from Persian dialects, was Latinized to become *lily* or *lilium*.

Lilies belong to the plant family Liliaceae, one of our most important groups of flora. They are related to such important landscape plants as hostas (*Hosta* spp.), daylilies (*Hemerocallis* spp.), trilliums (*Trillium* spp.), red hot pokers (*Kniphofia* spp.), tulips (*Tulipa* spp.), and Spanish bluebells (*Scilla* spp.), and are the second leading constituent (after tulips) of the Dutch cut-flower trade. Holland has approximately 8,797 acres (3,520 ha) of growing area under glass devoted solely to lily production. Additionally, lilies are akin to such culinary staples as asparagus, leeks, onions, garlic, chives, ramps, and shallots.

Undeniably, mankind's initial relationship with lilies was gastronomic. Lily bulbs are composed of fleshy, overlapping scales, and generally resemble a corpulent globe artichoke. In 1937, British horticulturist Vita Sackville-West remarked, "the Japanese complacently eat the bulbs as a vegetable, much as we eat the potato or artichoke, but fortunately for us they have also realised the commercial value to European gardens, and the slopes of Fujiyama yield a profitable harvest of bulbs." On the northeastern Siberian peninsula of Kamchatka, the bulbs of *L. camschatcense* are known as *saranne* by the inhabitants, and constitute an important starch source for man and Kodiak bear alike. Throughout China (where they are known as *Paak-hop* or *Pai-ho*) and Japan (*Yama-yuri* or *Teppo-yuri*) the bulbs (and dried flower buds) of various genera are eaten braised, boiled, or steamed; in egg custards, soups, and *gammo* treasure balls. Dried bulbs are also ground into a sweet-tasting, nutritious flour. Among the lily species used as food are *Lilium brownii, L. tigrinum, L. maculatum, L. leichtlinii,* and *L. davidii.* Lily products can today be purchased for home use in urban Chinatowns or large Asian markets.

Wild lilies belong to the northern hemisphere, and have an astonishingly wide global distribution. They occur naturally in North America from Oregon and Washington through California, Arizona, and Idaho through the Rocky Mountains to the Appalachian Mountains. They can be found from southern Quebec, Ontario, and Nova Scotia down through the eastern United States to North Carolina, Virginia, Louisiana, and Florida.

In the Old World, lilies can be found in Spain through the Pyrenees and southern France across the southeastern Alps to northern Italy, through Greece and the Balkans to Turkey, Israel, Afghanistan, Iran, and Iraq. They range through Nepal, India, Burma, and Thailand to Azerbaijan, through Georgia, the Amur area of Russia, China, Taiwan, Korea, northern Manchuria across the Sea of Japan to northern Honshu, Kyushu, Shikoku, and Ryuku islands.

Generally considered the queen of garden flowers, the lily is surrounded by lore and mythology that dates to the beginning of human civilization. A bas-relief from Aswan, dating from 2500 BC, portrays a lily bloom, while a stele dating to 2000 BC reads:

> **The lily carved here is the scented symbol**
> **of Seka, who in life emanated only perfume.**

Frescoes on the ancient walls of Amnisos, the harbor city of Knossos, depict lilies, which became the royal symbol of their king—they date to at least 1550 BC (and perhaps as early as 1750 BC). On the Greek island of Thira (formerly Santorin), archaeologists found pottery shards with images of lilies (possibly *Lilium rhodopaeum* or *L. candidum*) that proved to be about 3,500 years old.

While red flowers (including roses, tulips, and pomegranates) from earliest times conveyed richness and opulence, the lily has symbolized dazzling purity. According to Greek mythology, lilies sprang from a drop of mother's milk spilled by Hera while nursing the infant Hercules. The story was changed a bit by the Romans—Juno was the mother and Herakles the infant—who called the lily *rosa junonis* (rose of Juno), a name used by doctors, pharmacists, and botanists well into the eighteenth century. Both the Greeks and the Romans crowned their brides with lilies to symbolize purity and fertility. In ancient Rome, coins were minted showing the head of the ruler, along with lilies, and the phrase *Spes Populi Romani* —Hope of the Roman People.

More ancient by far is the Old Testament Hebraic usage of "Susan" (Shusan, Shusa, or Shosanah), which meant "lily." Eventually, the beauty of the flower led people to name their daughters Susan (or a variant), and the word came to translate as "girl." Because the seat of the Persian king had the name Shusan, the name Susan may have had a Persian-Syrian origin. The Persian city of Susa (modern day Shush in Iran), is known even today as a city of lilies because of the large masses of yellow-flowered *Lilium ledebourii* and green and cream–colored *L. polyphyllum* that grow there.

The flower is also well-known from biblical allusions. Perhaps the most famous is the Old Testament verse "My beloved is gone down into his garden, to the herbs and spices, to feed in the gardens, and to gather lilies. I am my beloved's, and my beloved is mine: he feedeth among the lilies" (Solomon 2:1–2); scholars agree that the flower referred to is *Lilium candidum*. Other verses, however, appear to refer to lilies but are botanically incorrect. For example, botanical historians concur that the immortal New Testament line "Consider the lilies of the field, how they grow; they toil not, neither do they spin" (Matthew 6: 28–29) refers not to a *Lilium* species but to *Anemone coronaria* (whose common name in biblical times was "lily-of-the-field").

The lily came to be an important Christian motif with a dual symbolism. It was a symbol of the resurrection, signifying life, glory, and beauty, and to this day we decorate our Easter tables with lilies (though the species commonly used, *L. longiflorum*, is a native of Japan lauded for its easy pot culture). But the white bloom also represented purity: the image of a girl (Susan) with lily flowers evolved into an important Christian icon. *Lilium candidum* (the species name, *candidum*, translates as "shining white"), known as the Madonna lily, became the signature flower of the Virgin Mary. A lily set among thorns has become the emblem of the Immaculate Conception of the Virgin, and represents the purity she preserved amid the sins of the world.

This association with purity made the lily a popular motif throughout medieval Europe. Lilies (particularly *Lilium candidum*), are prominent in the Unicorn tapestries (ca. 1495–1505), which are displayed in the Cloisters Museum of New York and *Musée de Cluny* in Paris. Here, lilies are depicted with maidens and unicorns, and the three elements carry the same implication—chasteness and purity.

Lilies are also frequently portrayed on European coats-of-arms, and it is possible that they are the original royal floral symbol of the French kings. Botanists continue to debate whether the *fleur-de-lis* is the image of a true lily or perhaps a species of European iris. It appeared for the first time on the French royal coat-of-arms in 1179, and continued to be preserved as a heraldic symbol, first singularly, then in triplicate, upon a blue field. After the House of Bourbon came to power in 1589, people referred to it as the "Bourbon lily." Today many cities, especially in France, continue to carry the lily in their coat-of-arms, including Lille, Le Havre, Versaille, Tours, and La Rochelle. The flower is used similarly in Germany's Weisbaden and Fulda.

Centuries later, William Shakespeare used lilies in literary metaphors and similes in more than twenty instances. For example, in an early scene in *Henry the VIII*, Queen Katherine touchingly alludes to the biblical imagery of the "lilies of the field":

> *Shipwreck'd upon a kingdom, where no pity,*
> *no friends, no hopes; no kindred weep for me;*
> *Almost no grave allow'd me: like the lily,*
> *That was once mistress of the field, and flourished,*
> *I'll hang my head, and perish.*

From *The Winter's Tale* comes Perdita's list of requisite flowers;

> *Bold oxlips, and*
> *The crown-imperial; lilies of all kinds,*
> *The flower-de-luce being one. O these I lack,*
> *To make you garlands of.*

And while lilies were indeed significant literary and artistic symbols, they were not neglected by the scientific community: the bulbs found their way into a variety of traditional remedies and alchemical experiments. Seventeenth-century alchemists thought to create gold from lead with the aid of the golden-colored bulb of the martagon lily *(Lilium martagon)*. This practice is preserved in the German names for this particular lily, including *Goldwurz* and *Goldapfel*.

Chinese pharmacists made intensive use of the lily, particularly *Lilium brownii* var. *colchesteri*. The blanched, dried, and pulverized bulb scales were used as a sedative, to treat coughs, as a tonic, to cure lung disorders, and to ease urinary disorders, deafness, earache, nervousness, and flatulence.

Lilies had been introduced into European gardens by Crusaders returning from the Middle East during the fifteenth and sixteenth centuries, and by 1629 *Lilium canadense,* a North American species, had arrived in Holland. German botanist Engelbert Kaempfer was the first to bring plants from the Far East to western Europe, and in 1712 he mentioned eastern lily species in his book *Amoenitas Exoticae.* Swedish botanist Carl Linnaeus, in his spectacular opus of 1753, *Species Plantarum,* mentioned a considerable number of lily species, including several from North America.

Eighteenth- and nineteenth-century Dutch and English explorers brought more Asiatic lilies to Europe from their expeditions in China and Japan. These early travelers discovered that the Japanese had a sophisticated knowledge of floriculture—gardeners in Japan had apparently been growing hybrid lilies since the sixteenth century. The voluptuous Oriental lilies (including *L. auratum* and *L. speciosum*) arrived in Europe around 1850. At the turn of the twentieth century, the majestic trumpet lilies (*L. regale* and *L. sargentiae*) were brought back from the mountains of China's western Sichuan Province by dauntless plant hunters such as Ernest H. Wilson.

While many lilies have exotic origins, most are not difficult to grow. Generally speaking, they prefer a deep, rich, compost-laden soil that is water-retentive yet flawlessly drained. Stagnant water and rainwater that does not drain quickly can kill them, particularly during the winter months. Lilies are much more forgiving about soil acidity than was once thought. Gardeners with particularly high pH levels can use the species lilies to good advantage. Many wild lily species grow in acid soils in their natural habitats. *Lilium speciosum* and *L. auratum,* for example, require very acidic soils; they will fail if their pH is too high. In contrast, *L. martagon* and *L. candidum* are native to European and Mediterranean habitats, which have naturally occurring alkaline soils.

These regal flowers definitely prefer a sunny spot. This does not mean, however, that lilies can tolerate baking in the infernal summer sun. Areas with light late-afternoon shade suit them very well.

The sight and smell of lilies are indeed among life's real pleasures, whether they are gracing our gardens, cultivated in containers, enhancing our homes, or even embellishing our dinner plates. Lilies have endured for millennia, and, it appears, will continue to seduce us forever.

My lady's presence makes the rose red,
Because to see her lips they blush for shame:
The lily's leaves, for envy, pale became,
And her white hands in them this envy bred.

Henry Constable

Imperial lilies in a bouquet convey a message of majesty.
White lilies in a bouquet convey a message of purity and sweetness.
Yellow lilies in a bouquet convey a message of falsehood or gaiety.

Kate Greenaway

Within their buds let roses sleep,
And virgin lilies on their stem,
Till sighs from lovers glide, and creep
Into their leaves to open them.

James Shirley

Behold, with lively hue, fair flowers that shine so bright,
With riches, like the orient gems, they paint the mold in sight.
Bees, humming with soft sound (their murmur is so small),
Of blooms and blossoms suck the tops, on dewed leaves they fall.

Nicolas Grimwald

*To devise living pictures with simple well-known flowers
is the best thing to do in gardening.*

Gertrude Jekyll

Nay more than this, I have a garden plot,
Wherein there wants not herbs, nor roots, nor flowers
(Flowers to smell, roots to eat, herbs for the pot,)
And dainty shelters when the welkin lours;
Sweet smelling beds of lilies and of roses,
Which rosemary banks of lavender encloses.

Richard Barnfield

My beloved is gone down into his garden,
to the beds of spices,
to feed in the gardens,
and to gather lilies.
I am my beloved's,
and my beloved is mine:
he feedeth among the lilies.

Song of Solomon

Planted in order
By the sweet 'Rock Close',
'Tis there the daisy
And the sweet carnation,
The blooming pink
And the rose so fair,
The daffydowndilly,
Likewise the lily,
All the flowers that scent
The sweet, fragrant air.

Richard Alfred Milliken

Nature rarer uses yellow
Than another hue;
Saves she all of that for sunsets,
Prodigal of blue.
Spending scarlet like a woman,
Yellow she affords
Only scantly and selectly,
Like a lover's words.

Emily Dickinson

Every flower is a soul blossoming in Nature.

Gerard de Nerval

There is a garden where lilies
And roses are side by side;
And all day between them in silence
The silken butterflies glide.

Francis Turner Palgrave

Then cried great curly lilies slashed with brown:
'We stood where cloudy torrents thunder down
Slender, for ever wet,
From falls that carry cannonading trees
Through riven clefts, and the collapsing screes
Besiege farm doors on scar sides of Tibet.'

Dorothy Wellesley, Duchess of Wellington

The violet, and double marigold,
And pansy too: but after all mischances,
Death's winter comes and kills with sudden cold
Rose, lily, violet, marigold, pink, pansies.

Josuah Sylvester

The flower-beds all were liberal of delight;
Roses in heaps, were there, both red and white,
Lilies angelical, and gorgeous glooms
Of wall-flowers, and blue hyacinths, and blooms.

Leigh Hunt

My borders they should lie a little flue
And rear the finest flowers that sip the dew
The roses' blush, the lilies' vying snow
Should uniform their nameless beauties show.

John Clare

On Sundays those masses of flowers pressed round me,
Muttering, muttering too softly for me to hear.
Their language, in my inept translation,
Was thick with portentous cliches.

Edwin Morgan

There is a personality about the lilies as distinct as that of the roses. They also have their lovers, who grow them to the exclusion of other flowers — those who proclaim them the king of the flowers when roses are given the throne of the queen.

Alice Lounsberry

There is a garden in her face,
Where roses and white lilies grow;
A heavenly paradise is that place
Wherein all pleasant fruits do flow.

Thomas Campion

I took a day to search for God
And I found Him not. But I trod
By a rocky ledge, through woods untamed,
Just where one scarlet lily flamed
I saw His footprints in the sod.

Bliss Carman

My Garden sweet, enclosed with walles strong,
Embanked with benches to sit and take my rest;
The knots so enknotted it cannot be expressed
The arbores and alyes so pleasant and so dulce.

Anonymous

How could such sweet and wholesome hours
Be reckoned, but with herbs and flowers.

Andrew Marvell

I sing of times trans-shifting, and I write
How roses first came red and lilies white.
I write of groves, of twilights, and I sing
The court of Mab and of the fairy king.

Robert Herrick

The garden, it allures, it feeds, it glads the sprite;
From heavy hearts all doleful dumps the garden chaseth quite.
Strength it restores to limbs, draws, and fulfils the sight,
With cheers revives the senses all, and maketh labour light.
O, what delights to us the garden ground doth bring;
Seed, leaf, flower, fruit, herb, bee, and tree and more than I may sing.

Nicolas Grimwald

One of the most attractive things about flowers is their beautiful reserve.

Henry David Thoreau

I send the lilies given to me;
Though long before thy hand they touch
I know that they must wither'd be,
But yet reject them not as such.

Lord Byron

She is coming, my dove, my dear;
She is coming, my life, my fate;
The red rose cries, 'She is near, she is near,'
And the white rose weeps, 'She is late';
The larkspur listens, 'I hear, I hear';
And the lily whispers, 'I wait.'

Alfred, Lord Tennyson

O happy garden! Whose seclusion deep
Hath been so friendly to industrious hours;
And to soft slumbers, that did gently steep
Our spirits, carrying with them dreams of flowers.

William Wordsworth

I know a young man who won his sweetheart by the patience and assiduity with which he dug for her all one broiling morning to secure for her the coveted Lily roots, and collapsed with mild sunstroke at the finish. Her gratitude and remorse were equal factors in his favor.

Alice Morse Earle

But they knew they were on duty, replacing
The Rose of Sharon and the lilies of the field
for a gardener who never put a foot wrong.

Peter Porter

By cool Siloam's shady rill
How sweet the lily grows!

Reginald Heber

In the cottage of the rudest peasant;
In ancestral homes, whose crumbling towers,
Speaking of the Past unto the Present
Tell us of the ancient Games of Flowers

In all places, then, and in all seasons,
Flowers expand their light and soul-like wings,
Teaching us, by most persuasive reasons,
How akin they are to human beings.

And with childlike, credulous affection,
We behold their tender buds expand —
Emblems of our own greater resurrection,
Emblems of the bright and better land.

Henry Wadsworth Longfellow

Thy navel is like a round goblet, which
wanteth not liquor:
thy belly is like a heap of wheat set
about with lilies.

Song of Solomon

Go bow thy head in gentle spite,
Thou lily white,
For she who spies thee waving here,
With thee in beauty can compare
As day with night

Thou in the lake dost see
Thyself; so she
Beholds her image in her eyes
Reflected. Thus did Venus rise
From out the sea.

James Matthews Legare

I like not Ladyslippers,
Nor yet the Sweet Pea blossom,
Nor yet the flaky Roses
Red or white as snow;
I like the chaliced Lilies,
The gorgeous Tiger Lilies
That in our garden grow.

T.B. Aldrich

A group of…lilies,
seen by twilight or moonlight gleaming
under the shadow of a thin wood,
is truly an imposing sight.

Vita Sackville-West

Look at yon flower yonder, how it grows
Sensibly! How it opens its leaves and blows,
Put its best Easter cloths on, neat and gay!
Amanda's presence makes it holy-day:
Look on how tip-toe that fair lily stands
To look on thee, and court thy whiter hands.

Nicolas Hookes

*And because the breath of flowers is far sweeter in the air
(where it comes and goes, like the warbling of music) than in the hand,
therefore nothing is more fit for that delight than to know what be
the flowers and plants that do best perfume the air.*

Francis Bacon

Have you seene but a bright Lille grow,
Before rude hands have touched it?
Ha' you marked but the fall o' the Snow
Before the soyle hath smutched it?

O so white! O so soft! O so sweet is she!

Ben Jonson

Brave flowers – that I could gallant it like you,
And be as little vain!
You come abroad, and make a harmless show,
And to your beds of earth again.
You are not proud; you know your birth;
For your embroider'd garments are from the earth.

Henry King, Bishop of Chichester

A lily of a day
Is fairer far, in May,
Although it fall and die that night;
It was the plant and flower of light.

Ben Jonson

*When you take a flower in your hand and really look at it,
it's your world for the moment.*

Georgia O'Keeffe

Among the beds of lilies, I
Have sought it oft, where it should lie,
Yet could not, till itself would rise,
Find it, although before mine eyes;
For, in the flaxen lilies' shade,
It like a bank of lilies laid.

Andrew Marvell

Flowers…are a proud assertion that a ray of beauty
outvalues all the utilities of the world.

Ralph Waldo Emerson

The pride of my heart and the delight of my eyes is my garden...I know nothing so pleasant as to sit there on a summer afternoon.

Mary Russell Mitford

The strawberry bed, and currant bush between
The honey-suckle hedge and lily tall,
Yield to the shrubbery and high-raised wall;
The exotics of botanic fame,
Of which the lady scarcely knows the name.

Samuel Jackson Pratt

Flowers have spoken to me more than I can tell in written words.
They are the hieroglyphics of angels,
loved by all men for the beauty of the character,
though few can decypher even fragments of their meaning.

Lydia M. Child

To me the meanest flower that blows can give
Thoughts that do often lie too deep for tears.

William Wordsworth

And the stately Lilies stand
Fair in the silvery light,
Like saintly vestals, pale in prayer;
Their pure breath sanctifies the air
As its fragrance fills the night.

Julia C.R. Dorr

These flowers, which were splendid and sprightly,
Walking in the dawn of the morning.
In the evening will be pitiful frivolity,
Sleeping in the cold night's arms.

Pedro Calderon de la Barca

It was the time when lilies blow,
And clouds are highest up in the air,
Lord Ronald brought a lily-white doe,
To give his cousin, Lady Clare.

Alfred, Lord Tennyson

The commonwealth of flowers in its pride
Behold you shall;
The lily queen, the royal rose,
The gilliflower, prince of the blood!

Sir Richard Fanshawe

Perhaps no more beside a temple gate
Will I unfold my vivid purple stain,
Or wave against the breeze my coral flag
Across the Amur or the Manchu plain;
Nor on Judea's hills in vision see
The Angel of the Resurrection lay
Against a Virgin's feet a snowy spray.

But I, beside a river of the west,
Where Alders bend and purple Iris spread,
Will lift my orange petals to the dawn
And wear a Turk's Cap on my crimson head;
And Solomon in all his might arrayed
Of linen, flashing gems and scarlet dye
Shall not be robed more gorgeously than I.

Si Tanhauser

The modest rose puts forth a thorn,
The humble sheep a threat'ning horn,
While the lilly white shall in love delight,
Nor a thorn, nor a threat, stain her beauty bright.

William Blake

But who will watch my Lilies
When their blossoms open white?
By day the sun shall sentry,
And the moon and the stars by night!

Bayard Taylor

And the wand-like lily, which lifted up,
As a maenad, its moonlight-colored cup,
Till the firey star, which is its eye
Gazed through clear dew on the tender sky.

Percy Bysshe Shelley

I'll give to him
Who gathers me, more sweetness than he knows
Without me — more than any Lily could
I, that am flowerless, being Southernwood.

Anonymous

And lilies white prepared to touch
The whitest thought, nor soil it much
Of dreamer turned to lover.

Elizabeth B. Browning

*Delicious symphonies, like airy flowers
Budded, and swell'd, and full-blown, shed full of showers
Of light, soft unseen leaves of sound divine.*

John Keats

The blessed damozel leaned out
From the gold bar of Heaven.
Her eyes were deeper than the depth
Of waters stilled at even;
She had three lilies in her hand,
And the stars in her hair were seven.

Dante Gabriel Rossetti

The pensile Lilacs still their favors throw.
The Star of Lilies, plenteous long ago,
Waits on the summer dusk, and faileth not.
The legions of the grass in vain would blot...

Edith Thomas

The sunlight slanting westward through the trees
Fell first upon his lifted, golden head,
Making a shining helmet of his curls,
And then upon the Lilies in his hand.

William Ordway Partridge

A garden without lilies or plants of similar personalities is like one without roses. In excluding them, it has failed to touch the inner circle of aristocratic flowers.

Alice Lounsberry

Yet in the bulb, whose sapless scales
The Lily wraps her silver vest.
Till vernal suns and vernal gales
Shall kiss once more her fragrant breast.

Mary Tighe

Identification Guide to the Lilies

Lily Classifications

As with tulips, narcissus, and irises, lilies are categorized within a strict system of botanical and floricultural divisions. This particular method of classification was developed by the Lily Committee of the Royal Horticultural Society in 1964. These classes, originally devised for organizing floral shows and competitions, are the following:

Division 1. Asiatic hybrids

Division 2. Martagon hybrids

Division 3. Candidum hybrids

Division 4. American hybrids

Division 5. Longiflorum hybrids

Division 6. Chinese trumpet hybrids

Division 7. Oriental hybrids

Division 8. Hybrids not provided for in any previous division

Division 9. Species; all true species and their botanical varieties

Division 10. Miscellaneous hybrids; all hybrids not covered in the above divisions

Organizations

The Netherlands Flower Bulb Information Center
30 Midwood Street
Brooklyn, NY 11225
718-693-5400
E-mail: sferguson@fcpr

Easter Lily Research Foundation
226 Chapalita Drive
Encinitas, CA 92024
760-944-1640
E-mail: lilyinfo@aol.com

Lily Societies

United States

Golden State Lily Society
5605 McDonald Avenue
El Cerrito, CA 95430

Mid-America Lily Society
86432 Belcrest Lane
St. John, MO 63114

Mid-Atlantic Regional Lily Society
35 West Phil-Ellene Street
Philadelphia, PA 19119

New England Lily Society
11 Jade Hill Road
Auburn, MA 01501

The North American Lily Society
484 S. Mason
Harrisonburg, VA 22801

The Pacific Northwest Lily Society
3948 Timber Trail, NE
Silveton, OR 97381

Species Lily Preservation Group
15980 Canby Avenue
Faribault, MN 55021

Canada

Alberta Regional Lily Society
Box 3683
Spruce Grove, Alberta
Canada T4X 3A9

Ontario Regional Lily Society
676 Regional Road. 30, RR #2
Tillsonburg, ON
Canada N4G 4G7

Australia

Australian Lilium Society, Inc.
  (South Australian Branch)
P.O. Box 137
Balhannah
Australia 5242

New South Wales Lily Society, Inc.
245A Midson Road
Epping, N.S.W.
Australia 2121

New Zealand Lily Society, Inc.
P.O. Box 1394
Christchurch, SI
Australia

Web Sites

Michael Homick's Lily Page
www.oxford.net/-lilium/

Lilies, Lilies, Lilies (lily chat)
www.garden.web.com/forums/load.cgi/
favorite/msg012005266232.html

Dutch Flower Bulb Industry
www.bulb.com

Bibliography

Brown, Deni. Alba: *The Book of White Flowers*. Portland, Oregon: Timber Press, 1989.

Cavallo, Adolfo Salvatore. *The Unicorn Tapestries at the Metropolitan Museum of Art*. New York: Harry N. Abrams, Inc., Publishers, 1998.

Chancellor, John. *The Flowers and Fruits of the Bible*. New York: Beaufort Books, Inc., 1982.

Chin, Wee Yeow and Keng, Hsuan. *An Illustrated Dictionary of Chinese Medicinal Herbs*. California: CRCS Publications, 1990.

Crowell, Robert L. *The Lore & Legends of Flowers*. New York: Thomas Y. Crowell, 1982.

Dent, Alan. *World of Shakespeare: Flowers*. New York: Taplinger Publishing Company, 1971.

Earle, Alice Morse. *Old Time Gardens*. London: The Macmillan Company, 1901.

Facciola, Stephen. *Cornucopia II: A Source Book of Edible Plants*. California: Kampong Publications, 1998.

Fergusson, George. *Signs & Symbols in Christian Art*. New York: Oxford University Press, 1954.

Findlay, Hugh. *Garden Making and Keeping*. New York: Doubleday, Page & Company, 1926.

Greenaway, Kate. *Language of Flowers*. New York: Gramercy Publishing Company, 1884.

Grindon, Leo H. *The Shakespeare Flora*. London: Simpkin, Marshal & Co., 1883.

Hendrix, Lee and Vignau-Wilberg, Thea. *Nature Illuminated: Flora and Fauna from the Court of the Emperor Rudolf II*. Los Angeles: The J. Paul Getty Museum, 1997.

Hill, Anna Gilman. *Forty Years of Gardening*. New York: Frederick A. Stokes Company, 1938.

Hirose, Yoshimichi and Yokoi, Masato. *Variegated Plants in Color*. Japan: Varie Nine Ltd., 1998.

Hunt, John Dixon, editor. *The Oxford Book of Garden Verse*. London: Oxford University Press, 1994.

Jefferson-Brown, Michael and Howland, Harris. *The Gardener's Guide to Growing Lilies*. Portland, Oregon: Timber Press, 1995.

Kellaway, Deborah, editor. *The Illustrated Book of Women Gardeners*. London: Bullfinch Press Book of Little, Brown and Company, 1997.

Kincaid, Jamaica. *My Favorite Plants*. New York: Farrar, Straus and Giroux, 1998.

King, Mrs. Frances. *The Well-Considered Garden*. New York: Charles Scribner's Sons, 1915.

Koomen, N. J. (translated by Amstelveens Vertaalburo). *Dutch Flower Bulbs*. Netherlands: Roden Press, 1992.

Lounsberry, Alice. *Gardens Near the Sea*. New York: Frederick A. Stokes Company, 1910.

Marshall, W. E. *Consider the Lilies*. New York: W. E. Marshall & Co., Inc., 1927.

Martin, Laura C. *Garden Flower Folklore*. Connecticut: The Globe Pequot Press, 1987.

McRae, Edward Austin. *Lilies*. Portland, Oregon: Timber Press, 1998.

Morris, Edwin T. *Fragrance: The Story of Perfume from Cleopatra to Chanel*. New York: E. T. Morris & Co., 1984.

Phillips, Roger and Rix, Martin. *The Random House Book of Bulbs*. New York: Random House, 1981.

Phillips, Roger and Rix, Martin. *The Random House Book of Vegetables*. New York: Random House, 1993.

Robinson, William. *The English Flower Garden*. London: Arthur Sanderson & Sons, 1933.

Rockwell, F. F., Grayson, Ester C., and de Graff, Jan. *The Complete Book of Lilies*. New York: Doubleday & Company, 1961.

Sackville-West, Vita. *A Joy of Gardening*. New York: Harper & Brothers, 1958.

Sackville-West, Vita. *Some Flowers*. New York: Harry N. Abrams, Inc., 1957.

Shelton, Louise. *The Seasons in a Flower Garden*. New York: Charles Scribner's Sons, 1906.

Tabor, Grace. *Come into the Garden*. New York: The Macmillan Company, 1921.

Tanhauser, Si. *Songs of Horticulture*. Long Island, New York: George Flatlow, Publisher, 1933.

Taylor, Paul. *Dutch Flower Painting 1600–1720*. New Haven and London: Yale University Press, 1995.

Ward, Bobby J. *A Contemplation Upon Flowers*. Portland, Oregon: Timber Press, 1999.

Photo Credits

MetroBooks

An Imprint of the Michael Friedman Publishing Group, Inc.

First MetroBooks Edition 2002

Library of Congress Cataloging-in-Publication Data Available Upon Request.

ISBN 1-58663-548-4

Editor: Susan Lauzau
Art Director: Jeff Batzli
Designer: Jennifer Markson
Photography Editor: Wendy Missan
Production Managers: Camille Lee and Leslie Wong

Color separations by Colourscan Co Pte Ltd
Printed in Singapore by CS GRAPHICS Pte, Ltd.

1 3 5 7 9 10 8 6 4 2

For bulk purchases and special sales, please contact:
Michael Friedman Publishing Group, Inc.
Attention: Sales Department
230 Fifth Avenue
New York, NY 10001
212/685-6610 FAX 212/685-3916

Visit our website:
www.metrobooks.com